Illusions of My Heart

Michelle Spano

Love and my life

It must be nice to have someone in your life; I suppose I remember, those days; the good ones anyway. I'm drowning in this space I call freedom; freedom is just a fancy word for; alone, when you are alone. My heart longs for its companion. It rejoices when I feel two people in love; or in something special. How long is the wait this time? Perhaps the rest of my life? Is there anything one can do when one is searching? Probably, stop searching. I know she is waiting, as am I. It is all a matter when God and the Universe decide it is time. Time is a tricky little bugger, as it doesn't really exist. Motion is just one continuum. It's fluid. We never really stop. You may think movement has come to a stop, when even settled into bed at night; but it doesn't it just slows down a bit. This thing called time is movement, continuous movement. I suppose then, maybe I have missed her. Quite possibly she has passed me by. She could have been standing right in front of me, and I didn't even know it. In fact, I'm certain of this. There has to have been a moment where we two have stood side-by-side without even knowing it. That's God's and the Universe's way of making a joke of us. They know our heads are so far up our asses, we never take notice of the Gifts presented to us. Oh God this is craziness!!

How patient can one person be? Maybe I've failed in my patience? "Just be patient Haqiqah." He asks; and I moan and groan, like a baby! Even now, there are two young ladies together; I sit and watch their interaction with each other. I wonder if they're happy. I hope so. I see my life with that one person; so I know it will be. It is the waiting that smothers me. It is killing me!!! Still, it is somewhat exciting to wonder when, where and what will happen when we two shall meet. Will it be funny? Awkward? Silly? So many possibilities await me. This is what we live for, right? The wonder of it all. Let's face it, when we finally get it, what do we do with it? Sure, in the beginning we seize the moment. Passion collides and the ride is amazing and carefree, then reality smacks you in the face; this is no game, it is no fantasy, it is no picnic and it is certainly no wonderful movie. It is fun, exciting, and watery; it is also work; especially when one of the two is edgy. Then things change. One pushes one pulls. Nauseating!!! But it's worth it, right? Love is always worth it, right? It is when it's real, when it's true, when BOTH are in it.

What is that shift? How and when does it even form? That part sucks. Nothing sucks more than loving someone that doesn't love you back. It's so daunting. The thing is you don't even see it coming. It hits you like...well...like something that hits you!! But it happens all of a sudden, right? More than likely, NOT. Everything is a progression towards change, whether good or bad. We are just too blind to see the unfolding. If we were open enough we could see the unfolding. It is true though, LOVE IS BLIND. Face it, we don't want to see the change; the one that is not you. Oh, how difficult love can be. So why do I sit here pinning over a person that is in my destiny? Her manifestation hasn't even presented itself, her and I, yet I love her. Already even knowing how difficult love can be. I've been through it all yet I keep waiting for God and the Universe to let loose on this thing called Love; this – relationship. That sounds so boring, RELATIONSHIP. Yuck. It should be...well...I don't know, called something less aesthetic and dull. Being with someone, sharing your lives together; your sorrows, your happiness; holding hands, kissing, laughing, crying, making love is one of the most beautiful things in life; it deserves a better description a better name. That name, could attach itself to me one day and I could say, "Hey, look at me! I'm in a ..." Yeah, someday. Someday when God and the Universe say, it's time. Right now it seems nonexistent in the unfolding of my non-relationship or whatever we will call it.

Right now I'd settle for just a glance. A small glint of hope with her. Who? Her. The girl of my dreams. The dream itself. God and the Universe need to move a little faster. This bleeding heart is wilting, deflating but never hesitating, never wavering from having, faith. That's what keeps the flame of my heart moving. Faith. Faith in me, faith in my dream coming true, faith in the Universe and most of all faith in God. I just have to be...patient...

Floating on a cloud,

And when the dust settles, I will lay me down.
Hallow ground; take me now. There's a lesson to learn,
But not for me, I have not earned, my right; to
Surrender my entire being to you.
You are gentle, sometimes.
When you are really here, what will you do?
Float with me too?

This endless journey is so unreal, because I'm not worthy of your soul. Don't attach yourself to this weariness, unless, you wish – that someday all will not be hopeless.
Drive, love. Drive me into the ground – plunge me into the river and run around.
See me reaching? I want to turn again.
Turn with you until the end.
But is there an end? No, my friend,
just me and you rolling in the wind.
Cast me from your vision and leave me reeling.
Oh, Love, come with me. Come and be
delicious – make me burn in protest!
I will not suggest, that we stop, but make a mess; so our hearts can feel happiness not distress.
I won't claim to be anything, you can find the real me in your fantasies and Love this shell, this nothing; this particle of everything that exists.

Tell me, how do you like me now?
Conquered and tamed.
Does your flame still flicker?
Has it died out?
Shall I become that animal you Love so much?
How do you want me now?

Love, Love, Love, Love; so many things about you Love;
how to describe you with just one word?
There is so much madness in this world, which you and
I live in; that no one knows about; so we tumble
tied up and get those things called feelings and
"have-it-out." You and I Love, there's no denying Love;
we have so much to give; but it's never enough. How do
we die-down this fever pitch? Better off to leave it,
where it is; and Love, me, Love; and I Love you helplessly, give
you my time until time has no need; and melt away like
chocolate in our hands. Oh, Love! Love, Love, Love, Love
me Love. These romantic ties, that bind us with such lies;
lies beneath the salt – the wound's frantic surprise.
But it's comforting, that sting; to know that even though we
shift around, somehow in the circle, when it slows down,
we comfort each other, and together, we found,
this truth Love, me and you Love, oh Love, Love, Love....

There, are little, all these little things that mean nothing
to you but much to me; much to my surprise – I find
myself drunk, my heartfelt testimony; to you, dear heart,
whose heart is mine; while mine is tied up, wrapped up,
a gift for your soul. Imagine now, both entwined and
out of control; the windy city in our breasts, beneath
the cage, in a rage; of loving madness.

Say it, say it with all you have; dear sweet, heart
say what I am to you. But, if your tongue
must lie flat, let it be. I will not tolerate coercion.
You and your tongue must give me truth!

Let me wean into this thing I've missed; for so long,
my love, love has lingered on, Love, searching for the comfort
of your heart; its home, it is home.

How is it I can feel your breath, even when you're not with me?
How is it I can smell the lavender in your hair and see it, twirling around the curls?

How is it you always feel so close; and knowing you may be
Oh, so far away, is when I need you the most?

It is the distance between; it doesn't separate, it leads; us two, together, it has a hold a grasp. Gentle though it may be, strong enough to keep us from coming apart, even though we are apart.

The distance sees all. The crying, the tears that fall; catching them, dissolving; keeping us at peace. Love, Lover, my beloved, it is the distance that knows our secrets; it weeps but it keeps us, always close. It can't take away what we've done, but hidden between is the love that allows us to become, one.

You are not merely a shadow in my brain. You are real; as the sun and the rain

You are not a manifestation of my dream, or but a dream; you are real, as the moon and the stars shine.

You are not so far, as I can feel your touch on me, like the snowflake on the tree.

You are not just a memory, for we haven't started loves quest. But this love is true; as real as the pain I feel – when I close my eyes, and dream of you again.

Oh, take over my lifeless body;
because it is lifeless without you!

How many times must I search only to lose again; as the pain remains; hanging on every word – cutting my heart in two? Must I suffer the joy of wanting you? Can't I just forget those eyes; they hold me high; but I fall, always – again and again. How many times must I fall before I'm caught by your love?

Can you lose if you've never gained? What is this meaning? There is no meaning to this madness. Forever will I cry without fail, never once will my tears cease!!

Oh heaven, how does it happen, you hold my love and will not set her free?

There's nothing more that I'd like to do,
than wallow in this pain with you.

Where are you my love? Are you like me,
wondering; loving an image, holding onto hope?
When will this be real? My heart is filled with love, but
it's so painful. Are you out of reach? Are your arms
stretched out? Can you feel my breath?
Will we touch hands?

God, my friend, bring my love!! Free us from this madness.

Oh, my feeble heart, it clings; to nothing. But sometimes, nothing, is better than something. You know what I mean?
Oh, my feeble heart, she hurts.
So confused.
What to do?
Options are few.
Days pass quickly too.
Oh, my feeble heart, she is a fool.
She believes.
Oh, my feeble heart, she always hurts. Someday, she will stop; will she have experienced anything real? Will she stop, knowing she was moved? Moved to more than just tears?
Oh, my feeble heart, she will never stop trying, she must like all this heartache and crying. It makes her feel – something, it makes her feel….

I can only imagine the morning dew, must taste and smell like you.

Sad we will never have a chance to touch lips; though,
I can feel their softness when I close my eyes. How real it can
be, only it isn't you. One day, when we are someone else,
maybe then we will cast a glance, and smile. How will we
ever know true love? I suppose, it is within us even
without a touch. To never know each other fully, that's
the dance that excites us, for, we will always be perfect,
even without knowing who we are.

I sit in the field of whispers.
My eyes closed, my legs crossed.
I hear heartache, suffering, people bickering,
then as I cast out a thought of you…
I hear your voice, soft and tender; you whisper,
and I can hear you say… "I love her."
Me? I think, I hope. She loves me?
I sit and listen some more, but my ears are
cluttered with whispers, and they cling.
I can't hear you anymore.
I sit with my head in my hands, crying.
I try hard to hear you once more but the
Whispers of others are too much.
I let you go…
I hope, I pray, the love you have is for me.
So, I whisper, "I love you, my Love," and hope
My whisper is enough; to let you know that I am here
waiting for you to appear.

The water stays in the cup unless I drink.
The food stays on the plate unless I eat.
The sun stays in the sky until it sets, and
your love stays in your breast, your lips, your
eyes, unless I touch, kiss or look into; and as
the first three things are necessary to help
me survive; your loving sigh, your sweet – soft
kiss and your deepness are what keeps me Alive.

I think of you, my soul-mate.
I know you are unattainable,
yet I feel you time and time
again.

One day, my love, we will walk
together, hand-in-hand,
talking of Rumi; one day,
drinking tea, watching the earth
settle, we will be...just be...

Will it be in another lifetime before we meet?
If so, will you find me? Can it ever be, Our Love,
can it ever be?

Ride this wave with me. You won't drown; even for
a moment, it will wash you of all you feel; and when
we come to the end, let me ride you again...and again.

Oh, sweet, little wonder don't you know you've got
me all wrapped up in this madness. If you let go I may
sink into the craziness of this world!!

Love, sweet love, come to me, but walk
slowly, so I don’t miss a drop of you…

"There is so much more I want to do with you, to you." She said to me while I lay down in front of her, at her mercy.
The lights were low, the music play; some symphony of life.
"Do what you must, what you want." I said; eyes closed, warm, calm. Then I opened my eyes, and she was gone.

There is stillness around me, and softness to my body.
A sensation of warmth flutters and I feel, relief.
So many times I've asked, "Will I ever be with you?"
Now, today, this instant, it doesn't matter anymore.
There are times when we just know; we needn't ask for
Something that is already existent.
In this heart of mine, is you; you needn't come if you
can't or if the Universe hasn't allowed our love to
shine. You, are mine; always, within the sanctity of every cell.
My Love, I no longer wait, I now say, hello.

I'll do anything to make you stay with me. I'll
strip down, naked and run in this field of daisies.
I'll spread this thunderbolt of frantic Love across the
world. It will make everything crazy, the sun will
freeze and the winds kiss will become warm and
lazy. I'll spread you night and day crying out my
name in madness; it'll be so wondrous Pans
nymphs will cry out with sadness, knowing they were
never worthy enough, to even think, to have this;
purity.

Enter into you, in me, everyone falling at our feet from jealousy.
This crazy love affair will split all hairs, but none more
than yours; for me, swimming upstream, in warmth
and sticky lust.

Earthquakes will be had because of us. My love, don't
fight this completeness it's made from the dust of
all angels' sweetness. There is no resisting this; it's you
and me in togetherness, making a mess, and I have no
Intentions of cleaning up.

My heart is too silly. It's trying to wrap itself around you, when it should consume you, lock you, imprison you, make you its own and dissolve you.

You've kissed me in a way I've never been kissed before...
now, I can't get up.

I don't want to "think" you all my life.
Love, it hurts you're not in this light;
my heart. Yours to do with what you
like; I write this story all the time.

What is this I feel again? What is this, so unreal again?
Alas, it is love; but one that goes untouched! Alas,
this is love, dear love, I love you so much!

I want to walk around dizzy with your love; keel over and vomit because I can't get enough. I want to languish and become smothered, short of breath and lose control. I want to spin dizzyingly until I fall. I'm not afraid of this, because, I know one day you will be here to pick me up.

I don't know what to say anymore. I'm so displaced. Oh love, you enter my head, you stay; you're locked inside. How do I set you free? Me free?

I am the embodiment of all sweetness projecting outward; taste all my sugar. It's all and only for you.

You have an amazing smile.
It definitely drew me in.
Now, I'm smothered in this
thought of you. It's sinful.
I can't think of you anymore.
But I have to.

She put her arms gently around my shoulders.
Her soft lips just touching my right ear, then
she whispered to me and chills danced throughout
my body. How long has it been since I felt such heaven?
How long will it be, before I am touched so deeply again?

I know this love is madness, such longing, such sadness.
How long before she is no longer here? Leaving me to sit
and want and wonder? Telling myself there is no such thing as,
better than this.

But she moves me. Oh, how she moves me to pieces, rendered
useless. Who else but her could leave me in such a mess?
Could my heart really want this? Damn me for not living in the
truth.

And the truth is; I am much more than you, as is my love. And I
know I must set us free.

Tell me love, do you know me? Tell me you do, but tell me slowly.

Break down each word with a sigh, break down my walls come inside.

I'll love you with every inch of me; I'll make you crave this crazy lust infused energy.

How dizzy do you want to be?

Tell me love, what part of me do you need to set yourself free? I'll knock you down and hold you there, I'll make you cry, I'll make you scared. But more importantly I'll make you see, that you'll never breathe without loving me.

Where have you been all this time?

Hiding behind that fine line, of, “I’m unsure and I Love you”?

Stuck is your heart? How can that be; if It, beats until your chest

hurts every time you’re holding me?

Your fear is endless, but my patience wears thin.

Dear heart, you must lose that strong hold that holds

you down. Isn’t it I that should be holding you down?

That way I do, that way, you love?

If you can’t let go of your fear, then I must go.

Maybe, one day, love will trump fear, maybe one day

chance will take over choice. Maybe that day, I will

still be free.

Remember me, lying here; heart beating, chest heaving, sweat dripping.

Remember me, when you're with her, wondering why she doesn't know to scream your name, it's because she doesn't know the same feeling, that feeling you get, when you make my body shiver. Because my pretty little liar, only my love sets you free. You can pretend you don't know it's true, but deep down inside you know you're a fool; to think you could have such madness with her. Please love, don't despair remember me lying, heart beating, still dripping, I'm here.

Is there hope in this hopelessness? Will I ever know your sweet caress?

I must somehow find solace in this regret. I thought I would have found you dancing a top your toes, only to find I have not found you at all.

This silence in the darkness of my heart is haunted by a love that loves me not.

There used to be this amazing feeling deep within my chest. Every time my eyes gazed upon your face they had to hold back tears, my stomach turned, my body yearned whenever you were near. Now I think of you and I don't know what to do, my heart she beats no more; she wonders why and she starts to cry thinking of that night you walked out the front door. This heart of mine can't stand the pain the thought of you is too much. I think it is safe to say that I'm going insane I long to feel your touch. But this cannot be, you are no longer here, no body, no soul, no more; dear love how I cry, wondering why, it wasn't me who walked out that door. How sad to know one little turn could take you from this earth; taking you away from me from and all our dreams with only memories of our love.

Remember when we walked hand-in-hand? No? You can't remember those moments when we kissed. It seemed as if we were trapped in time or space or are we trapped now?

But you are there and I am here. Free, ever so free. Or is it you that is free, and I am trapped. This madness seizes all there is, and there isn't a whole lot left, of me that is. But whose fault is this? Rather, is there any fault at all?

Does it matter? Has it ever?

Oh, how I've gone mad! I saw you there behind the mist!
Or was it imagination that blew me a kiss? But does
imagination move with such grace?

How will I ever know without a view of your face? But, if you
were there, would you not shine? Your beauty is such, that of
purity, so divine.

No. I've gone mad, as mad as can be and I'll stay mad until you
set me free.

My love, if I may call you that, will I ever feel your soft skin against my own?

This ache burns my heart and soul.

You must feel something, anything? Please love, my knees are bruised and burning!

Can you not see each tear I shed holds a dream? This longing is suffocating holding me down and making me crazy.

In this frenzy, I've lost my way. What more can I do but surrender myself to suffering?

Do you know what you've done? How could you?

If I could tell you, this I would say.

You've taken something broken and made it whole again.

But telling you would make you suffer. You could never handle such a sentiment. It would be too much for you to bear. And I could not bear to hurt you, because I love you. So, I will keep this to myself and love you from afar.

When I'm alone I'm okay. I feel silent; I hear only the quiet, complete solace.

But, sometimes, I think of you and the quiet goes away. Then, I hear the sound of my heart beating and feel warmth rising. Sometimes when I think of you I feel I will melt, right there just disappear. I like the quiet but I love the noise.

Come; sit for a moment while I show you all that I feel.

Watch, as I burst, turn into dust; or maybe nothing at all;

just pure, peaceful, happiness.

Be free, as I drink from your peaceful being; your heart, your warmth, your everything; dancing, twirling, drunk and dizzy until we can no longer see you or me; just feeling the love of being complete.

I've never felt so trapped in so much emotion.

I'm intrigued; I feel if I don't tell you of my feelings

my body will shatter all its nerve endings. Something

Is ending. I hurt more than anything.

But pain is not my enemy, just a way to you.

And you're so tempting; please help me from feeling so

Empty. Controlling urges are calling me, sensations

Continually seduce me and I'll come for you, just set me free.

Tufts of smoke curl upward and float.

I love thinking of you when I'm like this, weightless, I focus.

I wish I could bring you into this discovery of sub consciousness.

I'd love to float with you, and show you a world you never knew, where the color of passion is wrapped in green, yellow and blue.

Allow me to take you high, take you under the midnight sky; lets

make the man on the moon cry.

Come, float with me; see how beautiful the tufts of smoke can be?

You are my "Love Jones", my energy.

Don't be afraid, because with me, you are free; free to float.

Suddenly, the world is spinning rapidly and going crazy, changing everything I knew that was amazing. Now, my life is slowly melting into something very hazy; and as I try to clear the way all I see is you.

And I don't know if my heart is telling me the truth. Because I'm still in love with everything I knew. And this strangeness makes me wonder, who I am to you?

I'm not sure why this matters because I don't think there is anything I can do; except to lose myself in this haze and one day, hopefully inside of you.

Don't wait for me. There are too many reasons why we cannot be.

You may be my destiny, but more than anything, we are a tragedy.

Always against time, always passing each other by; so, say goodbye.

But, don't wait for me. Find love in the heart of another, find love, and set your heart free.

Beautiful eyes, your sadness I see, it draws me close, where I will remain until you let me go.

But please, I beg of you, be gentle; ease my weary heart slowly, so I can find away to tell it, not to feel lonely. Know my love, that you have only my love, etched in my old soul. And I will wait with the urgency of someone who has one last breath, until the day we can be together, forever.

Every day I breathe you in. This is why my heart is so heavy.

Often, I ask myself if I need this and my answer is always, yes.

I'm constantly teetering on that line that cuts through confusion

and helplessness; or hopelessness. Either one brings heartache at best.

But I'll let this confusion continue and struggle, as I desperately breathe you in.

It isn't very funny when life is laughing at you, when all you really can do, is let the joke unfold.

And, I don't think I can take it, but how do I erase this, as life continues laughing, while these feelings take control?

So I try to make sense of this, but it's becoming very clear, that the earth is shifting balance and keeping you quite near. And I want to reach out to you, while I reach the other way, and I long to feel you next to me, but you never seem to stay.

So I'll keep this locked inside me while I try to keep you close, and I'll pray you stay forever no matter how it hurts. This life is sometimes painful, and my sacrifice remains, and I'll let life keep on laughing as I struggle to my end.

Is there anything more wonderful than melting inside of you? Staying there forever? Tell me, what harm could come to be?

This insanity tortures me, taunts me, and overwhelms me with its authority.

Completely, I serve my love. Deeply I long to love.

One might call me mad; but it's this madness that keeps me alive.

The nervousness ran out of me as soon as your energy ran through.

Being tipsy was just another way of staying calm, even though every part of me was completely ready.

Tension from intension made me sober. Although, with you, soon I was drunk once more. Well, not really drunk, more like, crazy.

I felt as though I would melt, and I was enlightened.

Still, you remain. I feel so helpless, so drunk; this energy consumes me, and I will surely lose everything.

One day I will find a corner of the earth for me and you, so we can dance under the stars in the light of the moon. Alone, but not lonely; forever charmed by this beauty; hoping beyond hope you will melt into me. I will promise you only what I can give and bathe you with love that is true. Dance with me, only with me until the sun takes over the moon and we can no longer move.

My love, one day, I will find a corner of the earth and I will love you forever.

I have loved you from afar, now I wish to bid you goodbye.

My love for you is like a Shakespeare tragedy, ending without

fail, sadly.

Each night I sleep without you only to wake with loneliness.

Time, my ill-fated friend, no enemy could be more merciless.

I somehow feel I will be caught forever in a world of pure fantasy.

I cannot allow myself to love a dream, no matter how beautiful; for beneath this dream is a nightmare.

I have loved you from afar how I wish to bid you goodbye, but again and again I find myself sinking in despair, caught between the ecstasies of fantasy and the madness of reality.

I will, I know, always love you from afar, so how than can I tell you goodbye?

I am left breathless within your wake.

I do not perceive this as a suffering,

but a pleasure.

I am giddy with anticipation waiting to

see you again, and when I do I am left

breathless once more.

My desire is to never breathe again.

I would be with you in a heartbeat; but the heartbeat you are settled on is hard to get to, because my heart always skips a beat for you. One day the rhythm of my heart will be in stride with yours and they will beat on as one.

I have but one request, to melt within you. To feel your heat generated by my presence; and if I should die in that moment, I will take with me your warmth and be forever covered with your love.

I have fallen in love, extremely in love, with your beauty alone.

I haven't even touched upon your other adoring qualities.

I'm sure I will go made for them too.

I have fallen in love with just once glance of you. Your beauty is

power; and I will go made with my thoughts and thunderous daydreams, which will cloud my mind, no doubt.

I have fallen in love and fallen hard, the pain is uncontrollable

yet passionately soothing. I have fallen in love, fallen in love with you.

Oh, sweet love, how I adore you; how I can taste you upon my lips, soft as a pillow, comforting my loneliness, feeding my otherwise starved attention.

Your brilliance washes over my lack of sense; it makes me whole, gives me hope; in an otherwise hopeless world.

But you my love, my rose; so tender is your heart, so fruitful; how I will nourish myself from you. Again and again I will feed off of your tenderness and my love will grow; free and wild.

Stay, say you'll be mine; tell all others you no longer exist. Oh, true heart I will love you forever and forever will be filled with all I can give, which is everything you ask.

Please my rose, my flower say I'm your only love and make a lonely heart happy.

It seems forever since our eyes have met, since our lips have kissed. My love for you grows wild; a flower that craves nourishment that only your wetness can give.

A lifetime has passed and my body grows weary, to see you at last, will bring me to tears; how can I live without the sight of you? One could die without a hug or two.

Will the time come, when my arms will be filled? Leave me no more, or I shall die where I stand.

Wake me with your soft whisper, your warmth, your beauty; wake me with your soft lips moving, slowly, until you reach that place where my love for you keeps on growing, keep me moaning. I want to moan for you, plead for you; wake me.

Come, steal a moment with me during the quiet of the night, you can hear the stars and moon in conversation.

They speak of a beauty so bright while it has the sun weeping quietly.

Come, let us wait until the sun must rise, maybe we'll hear her silent cries; oh, but I have a secret to share, for I know she will hide when she sees you here.

Because it is you they speak so fondly of, it is you, why the stars and the moon have desperately fallen in love...

Where are you? Are you somewhere sitting, thinking, the way I'm thinking; only of you? Do you wonder, as I do, what would happen if we were to meet? Does a part of you feel as though it belongs to me? Really, I don't even know who you are, but I don't care; this love affair with my heart is something cherished, and true. What is it that you do to me? Does it matter? Should it? Should I only care that my heart knows that it is alive? I think I would rather keep you a secret in my heart this way my heart will always know love.

If we meet I will do everything to make you kiss me. I will shrug off all your warnings. I will take your hand into mine and show you how beautiful this can be. I will convince you that there is no other, no other than me. I will sing your favorite love song, recite your favorite poem. I will make a fool of myself to show you I'm only a fool for you. If we ever meet I will tell you how beautiful you are, how those loving eyes pierce me to the core. I will do everything to make you see, you are the only woman on earth.

I can only imagine the warmth of your body next to mine; the sweet scent of your skin, the rush of how my body feels when you let me in. The desperate kisses, long, soft, inviting; the strength of your legs wrapped around my hips. The scratches you will make on my back. Stroking, squeezing, biting, teasing all of which will truly please me. I can only imagine the heavy breathing, the sighs, the strokes, the moans the wetness between your thighs. I can only imagine so that's all that I do.

My tears they fall helplessly for truly this is goodbye. I will weep each night desperately, waiting for you to return. One day my love there will be no more tears; only you and me in a love so complete.

www.ingramcontent.com/pod-product-compliance
Ingram Content Group UK Ltd.
Pitfield, Milton Keynes, MK11 3LW, UK
UKHW040557210726
13854UKWH00008B/1377